First Edition

ISBN : 9798860454927

Printed in the U.S.A

My Employment with the UMWA Funds for 32 years

Kyu Won Lee

Prologue

I worked for the United Mine Workers of America Health and Retirement Funds for 32 years, from February 11, 1974, to December 31, 2005. I was first hired as a temporary worker before becoming a permanent employee shortly thereafter. I was briefly an eligibility examiner in the central office at 2021 K Street, N.W., Washington, D.C., before being reassigned to the Johnstown, Pennsylvania, field service office as a field service representative. I eventually moved back to the central office and became an assistant manager in the eligibility unit, and then a manager.

I worked hard at the Funds as I previously had jobs which paid in tips, like a waiter and taxicab driver. I hated those jobs, but I had to make a living for my family. I learned the eligibility regulations well and eligibility staff frequently asked questions to me which provided a good chance to be more familiar with complicated rules that had changed or added whenever new contracts signed between the United Mine Workers of America (UMWA) and Bituminous Coal Operators Association (BCOA).

The staff of eligibility unit processed applications for pension and health benefits as well as widow's pensions and death benefits for eligible dependents. Once authorized, pension and health benefits began to be provided. When pensioners pass away, survivors' benefits are payable. Many inquiries from applicants, representatives of applicants, UMWA officials, and coal employer officials were received every working day. When I was the manager, I felt the strong need to act quickly on the applicants waiting for our actions. I enforced internal instructions to our staff to be accurate, prompt and courteous. I repeated again and again that our products should be accurate. I hated back logs of benefit applications. I offered overtime to the staff so that beneficiaries would get their benefits in a timely fashion.

I was promoted from manager to senior manager, to assistant director and then finally to director of eligibility in 1999. In that capacity I was responsible for the processing all benefit applications and authorizations. Several thousands of pension approval letters with my name were issued to the applicants each year for decades. I continued to get promoted because I knew the eligibility rules and regulations better than anyone at the Funds, including legal counsel. The trustees and UMWA officials recognized that I was extraordinarily excellent at ensuring that covered beneficiaries received prompt and accurate information throughout my tenure with the Funds.

I wanted to stay longer but I felt I was blocking promotions of my staff. Reluctantly, I announced in 2003 my retirement date as of last day of 2005, two years in advance. I was surprised that the executive director asked me to hire my successor before I retired. We advertised the job opening in the *Washington Post*. About 80 applications were received. We interviewed half a dozen applicants, some of whom came from other states and their air and hotel expenses were paid by the Funds. I hired a deputy director, Katharine Gagne, who was working as assistant director in the operations department, for the job under me in June 2004. She would have a year and a half to learn my job. She learned the job well and she became the director of eligibility later that year. I had the new job as advisor to the executive director for the final year of 2005.

Many things happened during my three decades' work for the Funds. I had difficult times, and good times. I have written about them in some of my stories. I can recall hundreds of my staff members who worked with me. I miss them, all especially those who have passed away; I wish all the best to those who are still kicking.

Work for the UMWA Funds – Kyu Won Lee

Table of Contents

Employed by the UMWA Funds

On February 11, 1974, I was hired in a temporary position in the pension unit at the UMWA Health and Retirement Funds located 2021 K Street N.W., Washington D.C. It was a snowy day and some employees failed to show up for work, preferring to stay home. Others arrived at work late. One examiner, Irving S. Rizzi, greeted me and told me that both the supervisor and assistant supervisor had not shown up yet. He lived in D.C. and walked to work. I saw through the windows that snow was continuing to fall. We talked about our lives while waiting for a supervisor to arrive. He graduated from Georgetown University. He was a basketball player for Georgetown University, and held a law degree from Georgetown Law School. I told him that I taught English at Naval English Language School in Chin Hae and taught at Franciscan Language School, teaching Korean to missioners from 22 different countries in Seoul in Korea. I also talked about my student life and my work at the Defense Language School's contract school.

I also told him I worked as a manager for Jhoon Rhee taekwondo institute for several months in the year prior to applying a job with the Funds.

Korean language teacher at Franciscan Language School

Linguist for East Asian Languages at Defense Language Institute

Manager at Jhoon Rhee Tae Kwon Do Institute

The Funds office building at 2021 K Street, N.W., Washington, D.C. I worked as a temporary worker, eligibility reviewer, assistant manager, manager, senior manager and assistant director from 1974 to 1989 except 3 years when worked in a field office.

Sometime later Jack Ratliff, assistant supervisor of pensions, arrived.

He asked me to wait a while and he went to pension supervisor's office and took the good-looking leather chair out and gave it to someone and asked him to take it to the new director's office. This day was the first day of work for the newly appointed director of the Funds, Martin B. Danziger. He was an Assistant Secretary of the U.S. Department of Justice before he came to work for the Funds as its director. Ratliff explained that the pension unit had been receiving tens of thousands of applications from coal miners for pension benefits under the Blankenship Settlement, a class action suit against the Funds. Under the settlement, those miners who were denied pension benefits under 20 out of 30-year rule which did not count any employment prior to 30 years from the date of retirement. Under the settlement any mineworker was eligible for pension as long as he had more than 20 years of employment in the coal industry including at least 5 years of such employment with employers who had signed a negotiated agreement with UMWA (referred to as signatory employers).

I was led to a large inside room with many folding tables and chairs. Some temporary examiners sat here and there working on pension application files. Max Pheasant and Harold Dickenson, regular Eligibility Examiners, acted as supervisors of temporary workers and they were answering questions raised by temps. At that time about 60 temporary workers were hired to work on pension applications. Most of them were students from area law schools. The work schedule was flexible, so they came any time and left any time and worked from a few to 7 hours a day. The hour's rate was $5.

History of the UMWA Funds Before 1976

The United Mine Workers of America Welfare and Retirement Fund was founded as a result of Krug-Lewis agreement at the White House in 1946. Subsequent to a long strike by the UMWA members, President Truman ordered seizure of bituminous coal mines, under War Labor Dispute Act, and Secretary of the Interior Julius Albert Krug was directed to negotiate with John L. Lewis, the President of UMWA for a contract. The agreement provided a Health and Welfare Program financed by operating coal employers based on amount of coal produced and sold. The agreement also provided a Medical and Hospital Fund and coordination of the fund and the Medical and Hospital Fund. Finally, the agreement required a survey of medical and sanitary facilities by Coal Mine Administrator, of hospital and medical facilities, medical treatment, and sanitary and housing conditions in the coal mining areas.

Krug-Lewis agreement, signed at the White House on May 29, 1946

The Fund opened its office at 15th Street, N.W., Washington, DC. Josephine Roche was appointed as director. She was a daughter of a coal operator and Deputy Secretary of U.S. Department of Treasury. She had served in this capacity for the Funds for decades.

Josephine Roche, the first director (1948-1971)

The trustees of the Fund authorized pensions, medical benefits and other benefits to miners, their dependents and their survivors in 1950. Over one million beneficiaries began receiving health benefits each year from 1951 through 1953. The number of beneficiaries dropped 987,432 in 1954 and further dropped to 595,960 in 1974. The numbers of pensioners in:

1949 was 27,240; 1950 was 59,482;

1955 was 65,624; 1960 was 66,721;

1965 was 67,405; 1970 was 83,590;

1975 was 83,590.

About 200 million dollars were spent for pension payments in 1975 alone. Over 100 million dollars were spent for health benefits in this year. Since the creation of the Fund, billions of dollars have been collected from coal employers to provide these benefits for beneficiaries.

In the mid-1950s, the Fund established the Memorial Hospital Association of 10 hospitals in areas many coal miners' family lived, West Virginia, Kentucky, and Southern Virginia. The Funds provided hospital and medical care benefits to the beneficiaries in the coal fields from these hospitals in those areas. They also provided rehabilitation services in special clinics, medicine, physical examinations, and office care for severely handicapped patients.

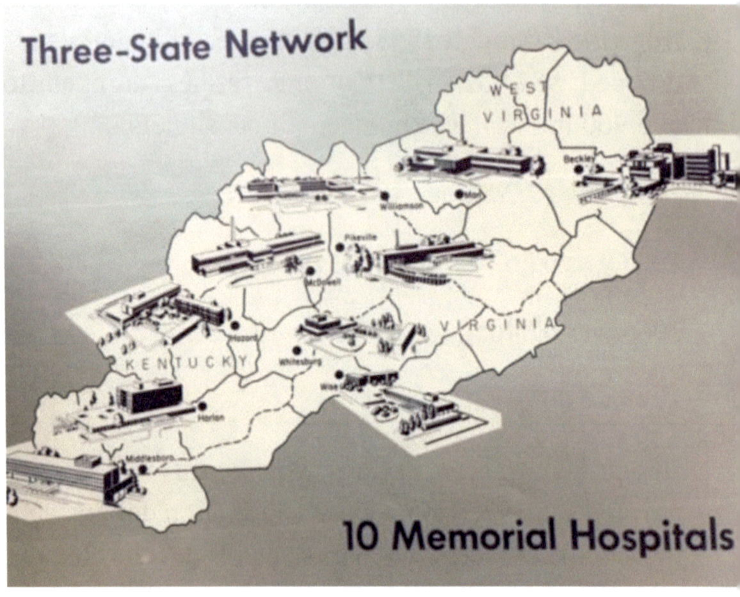

The Funds built 10 memorial hospitals and operated them in 1950s.

A Medical Survey of the Bituminous Coal Industry was submitted by Vice Admiral Joel T. Boone, Medical Corps, USN. to the Secretary of Interior in 1947. Warren Draper, M.D. was appointed as the Executive Medical Officer of the Funds. He was former Deputy

Surgeon General of the U.S. Public Health Service and he was Major General in charge of public health for the Supreme Headquarters Allied Expeditionary Force in England, France, Belgium, Holland and Germany during World War II. Under Draper many hundreds of doctors became the employees of the Funds and they worked in those hospitals. His two-decade tenure with the Funds brought him recognition and awards from the medical community.

Vice Admiral Joel T. Boone, Medical Corps, USN, (Ret.)

Blankenship v. Boyle, was settled and Blankenship Decree of Equitable Relief, signed in 1973, brought in

Warren F. Draper, M.D.
Executive Medical Officer

additional 19,000 pensioners. Upon this settlement widows of miners who would have been pensioners under the same rules were entitled to $1,000 lump sum benefit payments. Consequently, about 40,000 applications were received. The Fund needed to temporary examiners to process those applications. The settlement brought me as a temporary examiner to process the applications in this organization. And I became a regular employee and began my tenure with the Funds.

1974 National Bituminous Coal Wage Agreement created four trusts funded by royalties on coal production and contributions based on hours worked by each miner, to replace the 1950 Welfare and Retirement Fund.

Current Funds' office building at 2121 K Street, N.W., Washington D.C. This office was my work area as a director of eligibility, and advisor to executive director and consultant for almost a decade before I left the Fund.

Temporary Work

I was one of the few temporary Eligibility Examiners who worked like full time employees for seven hours a day and five days a week. We worked on only Blankenship cases. Overtime work was allowed. I worked a few hours overtime daily and worked five-seven hours on Saturday as well. My weekly paycheck represented 35 hours of regular pay plus many hours overtime pay. There were two temporary workers who held PhDs. Some have a master's degree, like me. I put in many hours and naturally made many mistakes. Max Pheasant and Harold Dickenson put a high volume of pension files in front of me and asked me to re-work on them. So many mistakes were made on signatory status of coal employers. Soon, I was known as a good temporary worker as I put in many hours of work and completed more cases than others. As the number of new applications reduced, the pension department stopped hiring temporary workers. During the latter part of the year, I was one of a few temporary workers still working there.

Outing with family while employed as temporary worker.

Regular Employment

In January 1975, I was called by the Human Resources Manager, Sheila Green. She asked me if I wanted to be an examiner, a permanent position. I accepted it as that was my wish. Most of the temporary workers left because either they went back to their law schools full time or landed better jobs elsewhere. My starting annual salary was $12,000. Fringe benefits included health benefits, life insurance and two weeks of vacation leave, as well as more than 10 holiday pay.

The new director, Martin Danziger, planned to reorganize the company. Pension application processing activities were decentralized to the coal fields. Old timers (known as dinosaurs by the classified workers) grumbled. They did not want to be relocated out of the Washington, D.C., area. Those who wanted to be relocated to the field offices began to move out to the field. Appeal procedures were first introduced and denied applicants had the chance to appeal. Many field service representative positions were created each field service office and they also served as hearing officers.

Martin B, Danziger, the Fund's director 1974-1980

I was asked to check out some field service offices and choose one of them to be relocated. I thought of Denver, Colorado field service office initially, but I made a to Bellaire, Ohio field service office. Jack Ratcliff had relocated there and asked me several times to come there to work for him. I also visited the Beckley, West Virginia regional and the regional administrator, Dr. Chadwick, said he could offer a position at the Logan,

West Virginia field service office. I did not want to be relocated in Logan after I heard Logan was surrounded by high mountains and the sun rises late and sets early. I also visited the Morgantown, West Virginia regional office. I had an interview with the regional administrator Dr. Smith. I found out I was unwanted there. Dr. Smith asked me to consider other offices.

Paul Moyer who began working at the Johnstown, Pennsylvania regional office asked me to come to the Johnstown office to work with him. He was the health department supervisor at the central office for many years and heard about me. He was a veteran of the United States Air Force. His airplane was shot down in Germany, during the World War II. He came down in a parachute and survived. His hometown was Lily, Pennsylvania not far from Johnstown, about 30 miles away.

When my wife, Jung Ja Lee, and I visited Johnstown to check out the area we stayed at a hotel. We arrived there late in the evening. We went to the hotel restaurant and ordered New York steaks. They asked us how to cook them. We simply said "well done" without knowing the difference. The stakes came out like black rocks. My wife could not chew any pieces we had to forcefully cut the meats. We gave up eating the steaks and went to our room. We did not know then we should have re-ordered them. My wife could not sleep well because she was so hungry that night.

I decided to be relocated to Johnstown. That office is the closest field service office to Washington, DC. Paul Moyer has also asked me several times to come to this office. The regional administrator, Tom Berret, looked gentle and welcomed me. Before I reported to the Johnstown office, I was asked to train new field service representatives in the Beckley field service office. We flew to that office every week and stayed there for three days each week to train them. We had dinner at Char Restaurant. It was a fine restaurant and I liked filet minion and cream of broccoli soup there. Whenever I visited the Beckley field service office I almost always visited this restaurant for dinner. When I took my wife, Jung Ja Lee, with me on the trip, she also loved meals at the Char Restaurant.

Johnstown Field Service Office

In June 1975 my family moved to Johnstown, Pennsylvania, about 180 miles northwest of Washington, D.C. The moving company, Mayflower Van Lines, sent their employees to pack our belongings. They were surprised at how little we had. They folded our dishes and other things in paper and put them in boxes. They emptied our closets and put our children's toys and bicycles on the floor. The huge truck pulled in and took all the moving items into the truck and left. We put some plants in our Ford Pinto and left the two-bedroom apartment on Buchanan Street in Arlington, Virginia.

In the small car, my three daughters, Christy, Susy, and Fonda, were in the backseat and my wife, Jung Ja Lee, was in the passenger seat next to me. We drove it to Pennsylvania. On our way to Johnstown, I looked at my wife beside me and my children in the back, thinking they depended on me and they came along with me where ever I went without any idea of what they would face in a new place. I strongly felt a sense of responsibility for them.

We arrived at the Holiday Inn on Scalp Avenue. It was close to the townhome at Arbutus Village where we were moving. My youngest daughter, Fonda, was only three years old and very active. She ran most of the time. She fell hard on the doorstep near the hotel restaurant. Her upper lip was torn and bloody. I felt so bad and hated to see the scar on her upper lip.

A couple of days later, we learned the moving van would arrive at Arbutus Village. We went there, and the

Mayflower van was waiting for us. We got the keys from the office and we opened the doors for the movers. The driver and a helper began to bring in our stuff. The driver said, “You have only one good piece of furniture that is this tea table, and the rests are all junks.” He meant it.

On Monday of the next week, I went to the field service office, located downtown Johnstown. The eligibility staff worked in another small office a block away from the Johnstown regional office. About 30 health services employees worked at the regional office. About 10 eligibility staff processed applications for pension and survivor benefits. Paul Moyer oversaw this unit. I worked very hard and completed processing many cases. I contributed to the reduction of pending application cases dramatically. Paul was so pleased to see the backlog situation became manageable.

The Special Assistant to the regional administrator, Suzanne O’Hara Wadley Jaworsky Rhodenbaugh, came by the office and introduced herself. “You must be Mr. Lee. Welcome to Johnstown!” She extended her right hand to shake hands with me. She was pretty and nice. She was very outspoken and regarded number two employee after Tom Berret, before assistant regional administrator, Tom Fulton and field office director, Tony Skull.

Suzanne Rhodenbaugh came to the DC area to make a home with her husband and her stepchildren. She wrote, consulted part-time, and did neighborhood and political work in Takoma Park and Montgomery County, Maryland. In 1978 the Appalachian Journal Crossroads published her essay "Death by Computer and Contact: the UMWA Health and Retirement Fund," on the implications of loss of the miners' health program, and substitution of commercial health insurance.

I still communicate with Suzanne Rhodenbaugh who now lives in St. Louis, Missouri. I once visited her home near the park and stayed for one night on my way back from a business trip to Illinois. She is a poet, essayist, and critic, and published several poem books. Her husband, Tom Rhodenbaugh taught at the University of Moscow and had some contracts with the University. He was able to lead some professors and students at the university to meet some congressmen in the United State.

Suzanne came with her husband and Moscow quests to Washington, D.C., for several days every year last decade. She would call to have lunch with me and my wife during her short stay here.

With Suzanne Rhodenbaugh at a hotel lobby

Our three daughters got along with many other children in the Arbutus Village. They rode bikes and played in the playground. Fonda loved swings and as soon as I got home from work, she pulled my hands to the swing sets. I pushed her in the swing as my first task upon coming home, even before I untied my necktie or changed clothes. We all were dressed up in the office then. I loved the time with her in the swing.

Susy, Fonda and Christy from left at Arbutus Village

The Funds decided to implement the mainframe computer systems to process pension, health, and survivor applications. The Funds hired the Price Waterhouse, a consulting firm to develop the main frame systems, the Funds' Health and Retirement Information System (FHRIS). The consultants and employees of our data processing department worked for the new systems. Several field service representatives were asked to develop computer input forms. I was one of them. I flew to Pittsburg and then to DC on Mondays and flew back home on Fridays. I took a small commuter plane from Johnstown to Pittsburg and took a jet to Washington D.C. I loved riding a small, 12-seaters plane between Johnstown and Pittsburg because I could see the white clouds that were like cotton balls and the land below better. I liked staying in a good hotel and had dinner at good restaurants in Washington, D.C. We worked at the central office this way for one and a half months.

The new mainframe computer system, Fund's Health and Retirement Information Systems (FHRIS) were developed and all field service representatives had one-week training at a place in Maryland, near Washington, D.C. Many attendees had trouble understanding the new systems. All eligibility staff of the central office and field service offices spent time together here. I noticed Robert T. "Bob" Boylan (1912-2004) and Paul Moyer got together a lot on break time.

Robert T. Boylan (sitting) discussed edibility issue with Paul Moyer (standing)

They seemed to enjoy the time together. Boylan was nice to me and prepared a nice letter and placed it in my human resources personnel files.

Boylan, former executive director of the Funds, died on his 83rd birthday, January 21, 2004, of melanoma at his home in Bethesda. I attended funeral services. Then the Employer Trustee, Joseph Brennan told me he would be there, but he failed to show up. He spent 35 years administering the retirement fund since its founding in 1947. He retired in 1983.

Boylan was born in Scranton, Pennsylvania, to a family with a long history in mining and union activism. His grandfather, Thomas P. Boylan, helped organize Pennsylvania miners in the 19th Century. His father, who also worked in the mines, achieved national prominence as president of the United Mine Workers' Local No. 1, and was an associate of United Mine Workers President John L. Lewis. Boylan graduated from the University of Pennsylvania.

I saw a sculpture standing in front of the building in which we had training; it was a work of Joan Danziger. Director Martin Danziger's wife was a nationally known sculptor. I heard that her sculptures stood in many government buildings in Washington, D.C., as well as the New Orleans Museum of Art, the Smithsonian American Art Museum, and Susquehanna Art Museum. She started as a painter but moved quickly into creating vividly colored sculpture from wood, mixed metal armature, resin, cello-clay, colored glass, and paint.

John Washburn visited me and we spent time together exchanging stories how we lived after we left Defense Language Institute's contract school where he was in charge of Spanish language group and I was in charge of East Asian Language Group, supervising Korean, Japanese, Tagalog and Chinese. Washburn's hometown was Vermont, and his family was a well to do. His father was a lawyer from Harvard and worked as Vice President of General Foods. His close relatives were mostly lawyers and medical doctors. He was pressured to go to a law school or medical school by his parents. He did not like it and he left home and got a degree in Spanish.

Washburn was disconnected from his parents and got married but the lady ran away as he lived so poorly. He went to Chile and taught at a university. He met a lady, Matta, and they got married. They came to Washington, D.C., and he got a job at the Defense Language School's contract school as a linguist in Spanish Department. We both got laid off in 1973 when the school was closed.

Washburn had an old car and lived in a basement apartment off Connecticut Avenue, Washington, D.C., near the National Zoo. We maintained our friendships. Several years later, he contacted me and asked me to visit him in his summer home by the Champlain Lake in Vermont. His parents passed away and he was inherited with one of summer home and some money. Their father has lots of antique items stored in a huge barn next to their stone house they built and lived in the countryside of Vermont. The street going to the house was named Stone Hours Street. The stone house was given to his brother who was a pastor with 5 children.

My wife and I visited Washburn's summer home, and we were so happy to learn that he and his wife lived comfortably. They had a home in Washington, D.C. and they lived here. They spent summer months from May through August in their summer home. They sometimes went to Chile to spend the winter months as it was summer there.

Washburn converted the summer home to a year-round home. They tore down the old home and built a log house with three bedrooms. We were invited to spend several days or one week almost every summer thereafter. We took our daughters and grandkids there too.

The house has a big master bedroom with a bathroom in one side and after that a kitchen and living room with fireplace in the middle. The second and third bedrooms are located on the other side with another bathroom. We used them when we visited there. We enjoyed the visits for many years.

Our second granddaughter, Morgan Newcomb, loved there and we took her there with my wife and I once. She loved swimming in deep clean water and kayaking.

Morgan at John Washburn's home, kayaking

The new systems were implemented in each of the field service offices. We had all kinds of problems at first in using the systems. Many rejections occurred when computer forms were processed. We had long lists of error messages, and many staff members did not know how to correct them. I was asked to help them out by visiting other field service offices.

I made several trips to Birmingham, Alabama regional office which encompassed the southeastern United States from South Carolina to Louisiana. The regional administrator was Dr. Wylie Slagel. Like many other regional administrators at the time, she was a medical doctor. One night, she invited me for dinner. We sat at a table where lots of silverwares were lined up and lots of glasses and cups on top of a white tablecloth. She suggested a lobster tail dinner. I did not know how to use the silverware. She kindly picked up utensils one by one and demonstrated how to use them. The waiter asked what kind of wine I liked but I did not know anything about wines. I asked her to order the same kind as she had ordered. She wrote about my visit in her regional newsletter, commenting favorably about my assistance to her staff. I still communicate with her. She lives in a beautiful home by the Lake Michigan.

Jung Ja Lee and I bought a house on Hornick Street, Richland area in Johnstown, Pennsylvania in 1976. It was our first home in the United States. It was a grey brick home with three bedrooms. It stood on a hill and looked like one story from front but two stories from behind. My wife and I used the master bedroom, Christy, our oldest, had her own room, and Susy and Fonda shared a room. The kitchen had a large window overlooking the backyard and the housing development behind it. It had a nice view of the neighborhood. We had a large family room downstairs with a bay window. It was a well-built home and we liked it. We bought it for $36,000.

We moved our office from downtown Johnstown to Richland shopping center area, a suburb near the University of Pittsburg at Johnstown. The office was located with ample parking spaces. My commute took less than 10 minutes. I would leave home about 8:45 for work. We worked from 9 am to 5 pm. We worked 7 hours a day and had an hour lunch. I always came home for lunch to eat the hot Korean meals that my wife prepared for me. I came home from work by 5:10 pm.

The staff of eligibility services consisted of one FSR I, a non-classified job, and nine classified jobs of three FSR IIs, three FSR IIIs, and three office assistants. Paul Moyer, the Benefits Specialist, was in charge of the eligibility section and he had a secretary, Mary Wojec. I was one of the FSR IIs. The FSR I, Joe Andrasko was supposed to supervise us. He was a miner who lost one leg in a mine accident. He had his own office and all other field service representatives worked in a big room. Office assistants worked in open spaces.

FSRs took application files from filing cabinets and reviewed them to approve or deny. We used form letters with some modifications to communicate with applicants. Letters were typed by OAs who handled application files and sent approved ones to the Central Office in DC by mail. As I worked harder, I processed more cases than others. My co-workers did not like it, but Paul loved it as he was very concerned about backlog situations. One time he noted too many survivor applications to be worked on. They were filed in several filing cabinets. It did not take much time for me to process those applications. I took care of them in a few weeks. At the end of the day, Paul went to the filing cabinets to check how many application files were still there to be worked on. He showed his smile noting the volume of applications shrunk dramatically.

Joe Andrasko was unable to answer the questions raised by FSRs and he called me in his office and asked me for resolutions. He was a nice gentleman but could not hold that position. He resigned when he got sick. Paul promoted me to that position. I had my own office with a bigger desk. I knew the eligibility regulations better than anyone there. Staff brought their questions to me, and I provided the answers. I sensed FSR IIs and FSR IIIs did not like me merely because I became their supervisor. In fact, I missed free little talks among staff in the big room office. The pay raise for FSR I was not that great. Actually, the pay I brought home was less as no overtime pay was with supervisors. Paul's secretary assisted me as well. She prepared coffee for me and she served my visitors with teas also.

Unfortunately, our secretary was not getting along with other clerks. Cindy Ramous did not like her and complained to me that the secretary talked with her friends too much and did not work enough. Cindy was an excellent employee, and her work was neat.

My office at Johnstown field service office

Eligibility staff gave birthday party for Christine Simmons

The regional administrator, Tom Berret, had a huge office. His desk was big, and his office was equipped with leather sofas and chairs. He had a special assistant and a secretary. He always came in the office late and stayed late. He was on the phone most of the time. Only Paul Moyer, among the eligible staff, ever visited his office. All health specialists and accountants had their own offices even though they were classified as employees (not managers). They did not care about us and we eligibility staff did not care about them, either. The field service office director, Tony Skull was

Trustees, executive director and department directors at the party

After my retirement, I worked as a consultant for several years. It was part time work, once a week or once every two weeks. Later I worked only once a month and then ceased such work.

Figure 2 My last office as consultant with the Funds (Kyu Lee name tag in brown on the wall). Orchid by the window was there for several years with pink flower.

As consultant at work

Testimony on Litigation

Nobel Class Action

I was one of many who appeared at the third circuit in Pittsburgh when the Nobel class action case was heard. Trumka, then UMWA president, and Bill Williams, then employer Trustee of the Funds were there too.

We all stayed at the William Penn Hotel near the Court. It was such a luxury hotel, and the room was gigantic and the furniture looked very old and nice. Trumka is now AFL- CIO president. He has thirteen million union members. Former Trustee Williams was the Vice President at US Steel Mine before he was appointed as a trustee with the Funds, and I was told he had tens of thousands of acres of land in Morgantown area.

Garland Case

I was testified at the Court in Fort Smith, Arkansas. The Deputy General Counsel, Israel Goldowitz and one staff attorney went there with me. We flew to Twin Rocks, Arkansas and joined two local attorneys we hired. We leased a small plane and flew to Fort Smith. The pilot asked me to be a co-pilot and I sat down next to the pilot and looked down at the farmlands and chicken farms. The staff attorney of the Funds was afraid of in the air, and she closed her eyes all the way. The pilot radioed the airport to call a taxi for us so that we could leave the airport to the Court as soon as landing. When we landed a huge black Imogine was waiting for us. They thought we were big shots as we leased a plane.

I have visited many Courts to testify or provide depositions and I always appear there with legal counsels.

UMWA Conventions

Marty Hudson, a union trustee for the last 26 years, invited me to attend the 1995 UMWA Convention in Miami Beach, Florida. It was held at Fontainebleau Hilton by the ocean. My room faced the hotel yard with lots of palm trees and swimming pools. Beyond that was the Atlantic Ocean. I went there with my wife and our room had two queen beds. We had a balcony with chairs and tables. The view from the balcony was fantastic.

Marty has worked for the UMWA for over 36 years, 26 of which were as Trustee of the Funds. As Chief of Staff for the UMWA, he was in charge of staff, collective bargaining with emphasis on health care, designing PPO's, and drug formularies. He served on numerous independent bargaining teams. He designed the International Relief Fund that raised millions of dollars to assist miners who were out of work.

I have met lots of union officials, most of whom I contacted over the phone regarding status of benefit applications. I attended the Health and Retirement Committee meetings, and the chairman of committee was George Holupka from Pennsylvania. He respected me, and we became close friends. Many UMWA officials knew about me and approached me to introduce themselves. We had breakfast and lunch at the hotel restaurant, but we usually had dinner outside. We liked one Italian restaurant, and we had dinner with Holupka couple several times there. When Holupka reported the pension committee meeting at the general session, he recognized me. I had seen him at District meetings in Pennsylvania many times thereafter.

More than a thousand union members across the country participated in this convention. In a huge ballroom, the convention was held and many distinguished speakers were invited too. One of them was then United States Secretary of Labor, Robert Reich, who was a good speaker. He was very small. In his speech he said, "I will work with you in hands in hands, actually my hands and your hips…" Indeed when he put his arm to a tall mineworker, it would not touch the shoulder but hip of the mine worker. There were senators and congressmen who spoke at the general meeting and one, Senator John Rockefeller III (D-WV) was unable to come, and his lively speech was on the screen.

On weekends we travelled to the Florida Keys and visited the Southern-most point, Key West, Florida. My wife came back home after two weeks, and I stayed another week and observed all the events of the convention. When I flew back, I met a young lady sitting next to my seat in the plane. She and I talked a lot. She came down to Florida right after high school in Ohio. She worked as a waitress in a restaurant and played on the beaches in the daytime. She loved that kind of life. At the beach she noticed a young waiter who did the same as her. They dated while working together and playing on the beach together. They got married and he became a fisherman, and she became a photographer. She was on her way to her hometown in Ohio as her relative's requested wedding photos. We got in touch with each other for years. She sent me a photo of her husband and his fishing boat. She said her husband left home at dawn to sail his boat to catch fish. He came back home at twilight with the fish he caught. No traffic on either way! I also received a photo in which a huge fish she was holding on her husband's fishing boat. I have a very good memory of this first UMWA Convention, nice hotel, good foods, good people, and wonderful speeches. I felt true warmness from union members. I attended all the conventions continuously until 2007.

Fontainebleau Hilton hotel, Miami Beach

Mirage Hotel in Las Vegas

Caesar Hotel swimming pool, Hotel room

At lunch in UMWA convention, Lunch with UMWA officials

I have also attended UMWA District Conventions. At one time we attended the District 20 Convention in NC near Smokey Mountain. Some FSO directors were invited, and we had a good time together. District 20 President, John Stewart was very nice to me, and I visited his office to see him many times in Birmingham, Al when I visited the FSO there. He also invited his district picnics several times.

Conferences

I have attended conferences many times. These conferences were held mostly in Las Vegas. Other nice places were San Diageo CA, Scottsdale AZ, Hollywood FL, Lake Tahoe CA.

Conference at Caesar hotel in Las Vegas

Conference at Wall Disney Resort in Orlando, Florida

At conference at the Westin Diplomat Resort in Hollywood, Florida

I attended NCCMP annual conferences many times in Hollywood, FL and Las Vegas. At one time we had a conference in Las Vegas. I took a cab from the airport to Caesar Hotel. I left my wallet in the taxi. When I stood in line to register, I could not find my wallet in my pocket. I did not remember the cab number but knew it was a yellow cab. I called three credit card companies to report that my card was lost. We had VISA and DISCOVER cards. I presented my wife's credit card. The lady at the registration wiped the card and told us it was cancelled one. I called the company while I was in line a few minutes ago. So, we presented the other card that I did not report, and we got a room. I requested the cancellation of the other card right after the registration. The room was nice, but we worried about the lost wallet. I had all kinds of cards, driver's license, SSA card etc., in my wallet. I called the yellow cab company and reported that I left my wallet in the cab that took me from Airport to Caesar Hotel and the time of arrival. There was a nice reception for the participants. My wife and I attended it, but we were not in the mood to enjoy the food. That spoiled our stay in a nice hotel. I called VA DMV and got a copy of the driver. My wife and I missed the nice luncheon on the last day of the conference and went to the airport hours earlier. When I presented the copy of driver's license, the security man took me to an office. My wife followed me, and they stopped her. They began calling some places including FBI. They undressed me and examined my naked body and all my belongings. It took more than an hour and they released me. When I came home, I notified DMV, SSA, and other places of my loss. They suggested I contact 3 credit companies and ask them not to issue credit cards with my name or SSN. I cancelled my driver's license and got a new one. Two weeks later the taxi company called me, they found my wallet and sent it to me.

I attended several benefits conferences with the International Foundation. One of them was held in Lake Tahoe. The meetings were only in the mornings. On the first day, the ballroom was full with participants. On the second day some participants were absent. The meeting room was about half on the third day. They announced some gifts would be presented the next day randomly. Indeed, they pulled the winners, and they called the names and gave the packages of gifts. Some names were called but no one raised hands or stood. Someone shouted, "He is now in casino!" My wife and I drove around the lake several times. It was our second visit, and we had a full week there. We loved it there.

I attended a conference in September 1998, and I was asked to go there with my wife. We stayed San Diego Paradise Point Resort in San Diego. Bernhard talked with Russell Crosby, the Executive Director, and the company would pay for my wife's travel expenses this time. Russell was a world traveler, and he knew there were good restaurant at La Jolla, just north of San Diageo. He asked me to have a nice dinner with my wife there. He used to call me "Dr. Lee" as I knew the complicated eligibility rules more than anyone at the Funds. We made a reservation at the best restaurant there at a seat by the window overlooking Pacific Ocean one day. However, it was after sun set and we could not enjoy the view of the ocean at dinner. I enjoyed a conference at Lake Tahoe, California too.

Conference at Sandiego

Conference at Lake Tahoe

Trips to FSOs and UMWA District Offices

I made business trips to all field service offices, in Allen, Kentucky, Beckley West Virginia, Big Stone Gap Virginia, Birmingham Alabama, Danville, West Virginia, Evansville, Indiana, Johnstown, Pennsylvania, Morgantown, West Virginia and Washington, Pennsylvania. I flew out to visit them for many years. Later, I drove to some offices that were not very far from D.C. It takes about six hours to drive to from D.C. and I drove there many times. When I flew to visit that office, I had to fly to Charlotte, North Carolina first and then transfer in a small plane to Tri-City Airport in Blountville, Tennessee. From Tri-City airport it is more than an hour drive to Big Stone Gap field service office. When I flew there it usually took more than 6 hours. Don Bunch, Director of the Big Stone Gap field service office often came to the airport and took me to his office in his full-sized black Cadillac. Later I began to drive to field service offices in Pennsylvania, West Virginia and Virginia and I was able to take my wife with me for those trips.

I visited most of the UMWA District Offices in Alabama, Illinois, Indiana, Kentucky, Ohio, Pennsylvania, Virginia and West Virginia. I visited them when they had union meetings or benefit meetings in advance of mine closings in their districts. Several

UMWA District presidents were frequent called me about the status of benefit applications of their district members.

I had good relationships with most of UMWA District presidents. Lee Roy Patterson, then District 23 (Kentucky) president sent to a letter to the Trustees complementing me about my excellent work for the mine workers. Bob Phalan, former District 17 (West Virginia) recognized me nicely at conventions and ceremonial events. Mike Dalpiaz, former president of District 22 (Utah), now vice president of the UMWA appreciated my work and sent a plaque.

Plaque Mike Dalpiaz gave to me

District 5 (Ohio) President and board member were very nice to me and awarded an honorary membership in their district. One Local Union in that district awarded a plaque at a UMWA convention in Las Vegas.

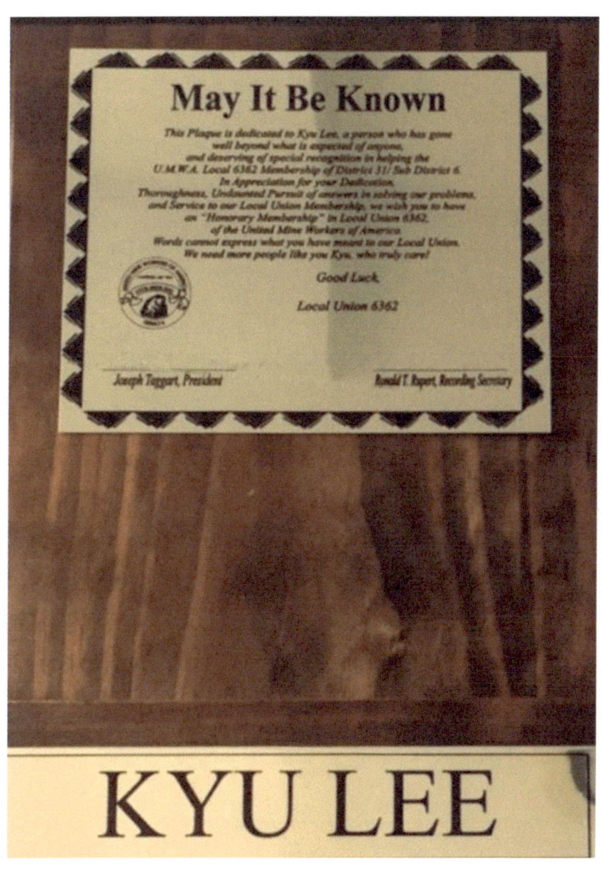

Plaque presented to me from Local Union officers.

Plaque presented to me from Local Union officers.

Ronald Rupert, a Local Union officer invited me to stay at his home when I had business trips in his area. He had a Coca Cola room that looked like a museum for Coca Cola. His wife, Karen had all kinds of birds in two rooms. They allowed their bedroom for us while we stayed there. Ron invited us for the Local Union picnic several times. At one time I took my two granddaughters with me for the picnic. We stayed one night in his home and the kids loved to be at Coca Cola room and enjoyed the birds Karen took care of. Ronald drove his car to lead us to the highway.

Ronald Ruper's Coca Cola room

Meetings at Mines

I made trips to many mines for benefit meetings with mineworkers. Once I visited a mine in New Mexica. The mine was owned by Teddy Turner who has real estate properties more than anyone else in the United States. I was amazed to notice his mine located about almost an hour drive from the city and nothing but forests along the way there. My wife and I were at Dulles International Airport to board a United Airline to Denver, Colorado on Saturday. An announcement was made that anyone who could fly the next plane would get free round-trip ticket. We volunteered and decided on the next flight about 4 hours later. The second plane was overbooked as well, and they put us in business seats. When we arrived at Denver and tried to rent a car at Avis desk. They already rented out the large size car we made reservation because we were late. They just gave us a luxury car. A Lincoln Continental for the price of large size car. We drove the car to a hotel in Colorado Spring, Colorado and we met Dale Morris, a senior manager, and his wife Dianne. The next day Dale and I went to New Mexica leaving our spouses at the hotel. We visited the mine on Monday and had a meeting with mineworkers. We came back to Colorado Spring and stayed one more day. On Tuesday, we learned the Pikes Peak was just opened on that day after several months closing for the winter. We went up the peak in our rental Lincoln Continental which was pretty new car with less than 10,000 miles run. We did not have chance to use the free round-trip tickets within one year, though.

Harvesting Through Patience

"Be patient, then, brothers and sisters,
until the Lord's coming.
See how the farmer waits for the land to
yield its valuable crop, patiently
waiting for the autumn and spring rains.
You too, be patient and stand firm,
because the Lord's coming is near."

James 5:7-8

Day 12

Harvesting Through Patience

James 5:7-8

"Be patient, then, brothers and sisters, until the Lord's coming. See how the farmer waits for the land to yield its valuable crop, patiently waiting for the autumn and spring rains. You too, be patient and stand firm, because the Lord's coming is near."

Reflection:
Patience is a virtue that many of us struggle with, especially in the fast-paced world of entrepreneurship. But as James aptly puts it, just as a farmer waits patiently for the rains to nurture his crops, we too must cultivate patience in our pursuits.

In the business realm, it's easy to get impatient when results aren't immediate. Whether it's a marketing strategy not bringing in expected leads, a product not taking off, or a partnership taking time to materialize, our instant-gratification mindset nudges us towards frustration.

But let's recalibrate our perspective. Often, the most potent transformations, the most significant growths, are happening just beneath the surface. Just as seeds germinate in the dark soil before breaking forth into the light, our efforts, grounded in faith and patience, will bear fruit in due season.

Remember, God's timing is impeccable. So even if the "harvest" in your entrepreneurial venture seems delayed, it's being divinely orchestrated. Stay patient, keep nurturing your goals, and believe in the abundance that's to come.

Action Steps:
1. Reflect and Record: Journal about a past situation where patience led to unexpected blessings or success. Let this serve as a reminder in moments of impatience.

2. Seek Wisdom: If you're growing impatient with a specific aspect of your business, seek guidance. It could be from a mentor, a fellow entrepreneur, or through prayer.

3. Celebrate Small Wins: While waiting for the significant harvest, don't forget to celebrate the small milestones. They are stepping stones to your grand vision.

Prayer:
Lord, grant me the patience to trust in Your timing, to understand that every delay is a divine setup for a greater harvest. Let my heart be still, knowing that just as You care for the lilies and the birds, You are meticulously orchestrating my journey. In Jesus' name, Amen.

Empowering Others Through Servant Leadership

"For even the Son of Man did not come to be served, but to serve, and to give his life as a ransom for many."

James 5:7-8

Day 13

Empowering Others Through Servant Leadership

Mark 10:45

"For even the Son of Man did not come to be served,
but to serve, and to give his life as a ransom for many."

Reflection:
True leadership, the kind that leaves an indelible mark, is not about wielding power or establishing dominance. It's about service. Jesus, the King of Kings, demonstrated this most profoundly. He washed the feet of His disciples, performed miracles to heal and comfort, and ultimately gave His life for our redemption.

In the realm of entrepreneurship, servant leadership means prioritizing the well-being and success of those you lead over your own ambitions. It's about recognizing the potential in others and empowering them to rise to their best selves. A servant leader understands that their true success is measured not by personal gains but by the growth and fulfillment of their team and community.

But, how does one become a servant leader? By embracing humility, actively listening, and putting the needs of others first. By being willing to roll up your sleeves and work alongside your team. By being the kind of leader who uplifts, encourages, and mentors.

Today, as you navigate your entrepreneurial journey, remember that the most lasting legacies are built on the foundation of service. Empower, serve, and lead with a heart that mirrors Christ's.

Action Steps:
1.**Reflect on Your Leadership:** Take a few moments to assess your leadership style. Are there areas where you can be more of a servant leader?

2.**Acknowledge and Appreciate:** Recognize the hard work and dedication of your team or those around you. A simple acknowledgment can be a powerful motivator.

3.**Learn Continuously:** Dive into resources that expound on servant leadership. The more you learn, the more you can embody these principles in your daily life.

Prayer:
Lord Jesus, You exemplified what it means to be a true leader. Instill in me the heart of a servant leader. May I always prioritize the well-being of others, leading with humility, grace, and love. Help me to mirror Your love in my interactions, fostering an environment of growth, empowerment, and mutual respect. In Your name, I pray, Amen.

Valuing Time and Setting Good Boundaries

"To everything there is a season,
and a time to every purpose
under the heaven: A time to be
born, and a time to die;
a time to plant, and a time to
pluck up that which is planted..."

Ecclesiastes 3:1-8
(A Time for Everything)

Day 14

Valuing Time and Setting Good Boundaries

Ecclesiastes 3:1-8 (A Time for Everything)

"To everything there is a season, and a time to every purpose
under the heaven: A time to be born, and a time to die;
a time to plant, and a time to pluck up that which is planted..."

Reflection:
As entrepreneurs and bearers of Christ's mission, our days can often feel like a sprint against time. The wise words of Ecclesiastes remind us that time is not just a resource to be managed, but a divine gift to be honored. Each moment carries with it an opportunity for a specific purpose, calling for discernment and intentionality.

In the relentless pace of growing a business, it can be challenging to maintain healthy boundaries, to say 'no,' or to recognize when to pause. Yet, understanding the rhythm of God's timing is crucial. It teaches us that there is a season for pushing forward with intensity, and there is a season for rest and reflection.

Valuing time means respecting its sanctity and setting boundaries that align with God's will. It means trusting that our Heavenly Father has ordained a time for every aspect of our life and work. Our role is to navigate these seasons with wisdom, aligning our actions with the divine cadence set before us.

Action Steps:
1. Assess Your Schedule: Take a close look at your commitments. Are there areas where you need to set or reinforce boundaries to respect God's timing?

2. Pray for Discernment: Seek God's guidance to understand what season you are currently in and what actions are required of you in this season.

3. Embrace Each Season: Whether a time to work diligently or a time to rest, embrace it fully, knowing that God's timing is perfect.

Prayer:
Lord, grant me the wisdom to value the time You have given me. Help me to recognize and respect the seasons of my life and business, setting boundaries that honor You. Teach me to discern the purpose for each time You set before me, and give me the strength to uphold these seasons with grace. In Jesus' name, Amen.

Embracing The Divine Design

"For I know the plans
I have for you,"
declares the LORD,"
plans to prosper you
and not to harm you,
plans to give you hope
and a future."

Jeremiah 29:11

Day 15

Embracing The Divine Design

Jeremiah 29:11

"For I know the plans I have for you," declares the LORD, "
plans to prosper you and not to harm you,
plans to give you hope and a future."

Reflection:
Every venture, every dream, and every aspiration you hold has been carefully woven into the divine blueprint for your life. God, the master architect, has crafted a unique plan for you, infused with purpose and promise.

Jeremiah's words are a powerful reminder that our endeavors are not just about financial gain or worldly recognition. They are about aligning with God's greater plan - a plan that promises prosperity, hope, and a future. It's easy to become so engrossed in our daily tasks, targets, and challenges that we lose sight of the bigger picture. But there's immense peace in knowing that God's plan for our business and our life is always for our ultimate good.

Your entrepreneurial journey isn't just about building a successful enterprise; it's about discovering and embracing God's divine design for your life. Every challenge you face, every decision you make, and every success you celebrate is a part of His beautiful tapestry for you.

Action Steps:
1.Seek Clarity: Take a moment to pray and meditate on Jeremiah 29:11. Ask God to reveal His plans and purposes for your business.

2.Embrace the Journey: Instead of resisting challenges or setbacks, see them as part of God's refining process, shaping you for your divine destiny.

3.Milestones: Recognize and celebrate the milestones in your entrepreneurial journey, acknowledging God's hand in your successes.

Prayer:
Heavenly Father, I thank You for the divine plan You have for my life and my business. Help me to always align my aspirations with Your purpose. As I journey through the ups and downs, may I always remember that You are guiding me towards a future filled with hope. In Jesus' name, Amen.

Fueling Forward with Faithful Finances

"Honor the Lord with your
wealth, with the firstfruits
of all your crops; then your
barns will be filled to
overflowing, and
your vats will brim over
with new wine."

Proverbs 3:9-10

Day 16

Fueling Forward with Faithful Finances

Proverbs 3:9-10

"Honor the Lord with your wealth, with the firstfruits of all your crops; then your barns will be filled to overflowing, and your vats will brim over with new wine."

Reflection:
Money and wealth, often regarded with caution in spiritual discourse, are actually tools gifted to us by God. How we steward them reveals much about our heart and our understanding of God's kingdom. The scripture from Proverbs is a timeless principle that offers profound wisdom for faith-driven entrepreneurs: When we prioritize God in our financial decisions and honor Him with our wealth, He promises not just provision but abundance.

For the entrepreneur, this isn't just about tithing, but about integrating godly financial principles into the very fabric of their business models, decision-making processes, and investment choices. By putting God first in your finances, you invite His blessings and guidance into every aspect of your enterprise.

This approach to finances allows you to operate from a place of trust, knowing that when you honor God, He ensures that your resources are not just sufficient but abundant. You're not just working for profit but to propel God's purposes on Earth.

Action Steps:
1.Budget with God: Start your financial planning by allocating a portion to honor God. This sets a tone of trust and acknowledgment of His provision.

2.Pray Over Financial Decisions: Before making significant financial decisions, take them to prayer. Seek God's wisdom and guidance.

3.Seek Financial Wisdom: Regularly educate yourself on biblical financial principles and strive to integrate them into your business.

Prayer:
Lord, I dedicate my resources to You. Guide me in my financial decisions, and help me always put You first. Let my business be a vessel of Your blessings and a testament to Your abundance. Teach me to steward my wealth with wisdom and grace. In Jesus' name, Amen.

Seeking Wise Counsel

"Blessed is the one who
does not walk in step with
the wicked
or stand in the way that
sinners take or sit in the
company of mockers,
but whose delight is in the
law of the Lord, and
who meditates on his law
day and night."

Psalms 1

Day 17

Seeking Wise Counsel

Psalms 1

"Blessed is the one who does not walk in step with the wicked
or stand in the way that sinners take or sit in the company of mockers,
but whose delight is in the law of the Lord, and
who meditates on his law day and night."

Reflection:
In the challenging journey of entrepreneurship, the voices that speak into our lives can significantly sway our paths. The first Psalm presents a vivid contrast between the one who follows the counsel of the wicked and the one who delights in the law of the Lord. It's a stark reminder of the importance of choosing our influences wisely.

As a faith-driven entrepreneur, your business is not just a means of income; it's a ministry and a mission field. The counsel you seek should therefore resonate with your spiritual values, offering not only smart business strategies but also aligning with the wisdom of God's Word.

Seeking wise counsel means surrounding yourself with mentors and advisors who not only excel in business acumen but also possess a heart attuned to God. It means forming a circle of influence that champions integrity, encourages faithfulness, and inspires Godly wisdom in every decision.

Action Steps:
1. Evaluate Your Influences: Reflect on the voices of influence in your business and personal life. Are they encouraging you toward Godly wisdom or worldly success at any cost?

2. Seek Godly Mentors: Actively look for and reach out to individuals who exemplify wise counsel, both in business expertise and spiritual maturity.

3. Be Discerning: Not all advice is beneficial. Pray for discernment to know which counsel aligns with God's will for your life and business.

Prayer:
Father, guide me to seek and heed wise counsel that aligns with Your Word. Help me to discern the influences in my life, ensuring that they lead me closer to You and Your purposes. May Your truth light the way in every business decision I make. In Jesus' name, Amen.

Unwavering Unity: Building Bridges, Not Walls

"Make every effort to keep
the unity of the Spirit
through the bond of peace."

Ephesians 4:3

Day 18

Unwavering Unity: Building Bridges, Not Walls

Ephesians 4:3

"Make every effort to keep the unity of the Spirit through the bond of peace."

Reflection:
It is my prayer that I would always see potential allies instead of competitors, to build bridges of collaboration and partnership. That my endeavors reflect God's desire for unity and peace among His people.

Unity doesn't diminish individual achievements or negate the importance of unique vision. Rather, it amplifies them. When faith-driven entrepreneurs come together in unity of purpose, pooling resources, wisdom, and skills, they become a formidable force for good in the world. They reflect God's own desire for unity among His people. that is the power of the mastermind and why so many successful business leaders are part of them.

Jealousy, unhealthy competition and envy will always slow you down and get you off focus. They bring confusion and give power to the enemy to hold you back.

Unity in the business world doesn't mean abandoning discernment or ignoring real challenges in collaboration. It doesn't mean compromising your faith. It does mean approaching partnerships with grace, looking for shared values, and working toward mutual success. It's about recognizing that the Spirit binds us together and that our combined efforts, grounded in peace and mutual respect, can achieve far more than any one individual might alone.

Action Steps:
1.Seek Collaboration: Identify potential partners or mentors in your field with whom you can collaborate for mutual benefit.

2.Build Bridges: Actively seek to reconcile strained business relationships. Approach disagreements with a mindset of peace and resolution.

3.Celebrate Others: When others in your field succeed, celebrate with them. Recognize that their success uplifts the entire community.

Prayer:
Heavenly Father, cultivate in me a heart of humility and desire for unity. Help me to serve others with love and selflessness, mirroring the example set by Jesus. May my business endeavors not be only about personal gain but about uplifting and serving others. In Jesus' name, I pray. Amen.

Harvesting Hope: Planting Seeds for Tomorrow's Success

"Now faith is confidence
in what we hope for and
assurance about what we
do not see."

Hebrews 11:1

Day 19

Harvesting Hope: Planting Seeds for Tomorrow's Success

Hebrews 11:1

"Now faith is confidence in what we hope for and assurance about what we do not see."

Reflection:
Every entrepreneur understands the value of investment. The time, resources, and energy expended today often determine tomorrow's outcome. But there's another kind of investment, intangible yet powerful, that every faith-driven entrepreneur must understand: Investing in hope through faith.

The scripture reminds us that faith is the bedrock of our hope. In the realm of business, this means that even when our strategies don't yield immediate results, or when the road ahead seems foggy, our faith grounds us. It reminds us that our labor is not in vain, and that seeds planted in faith will, in due time, bring forth a harvest.

As faith-driven entrepreneurs, it's crucial to remember that our ventures are not just about financial gain or market success. They are about the larger impact, the lives touched, the communities transformed, and the legacy we leave. These might not always be immediately visible, but with hope rooted in faith, we can move forward with confidence, knowing that our efforts will bear fruit in God's perfect time.

Action Steps:
1.**Vision Journaling:** Set aside some quiet time to journal about the long-term vision for your enterprise. What seeds are you planting now that will bear generational fruit?

2.**Stay Grounded:** In moments of doubt or impatience, return to this scripture. Let it remind you of the importance of faith and hope in your journey.

3.**Share Hope:** Be a beacon of hope in your business community. Share testimonies of past successes and challenges overcome, reminding others that with faith, all things are possible.

Prayer:
Lord, fortify my heart with unshakeable faith and hope. Even when I cannot see the immediate fruits of my labor, let me be confident in Your promise and timing. Help me to plant seeds in faith, knowing that they will yield a bountiful harvest in Your perfect time.In Jesus' name, Amen.

Positive Mindset: The Choice That Shapes Our Success

"Finally, brothers and
sisters, whatever is true,
whatever is noble,
whatever is right,
whatever is pure,
whatever is lovely,
whatever is admirable—
if anything is excellent or
praiseworthy
—think about such
things."

Philippians 4:8

Day 20

Positive Mindset: The Choice That Shapes Our Success

Philippians 4:8

"Finally, brothers and sisters, whatever is true, whatever is noble, whatever is right, whatever is pure, whatever is lovely, whatever is admirable—if anything is excellent or praiseworthy —think about such things."

Reflection:
The mindset with which we approach life's challenges and opportunities can be a self-fulfilling prophecy. Paul's letter to the Philippians is not a call to naive optimism but an invitation to a disciplined thought life. As entrepreneurs and kingdom-builders, the choice to focus on the positive is a conscious one that can significantly impact our trajectory toward success.

In a world full of negativity and cynicism, maintaining a positive mindset is an act of defiance against the norm. It's choosing to see God's hand at work even in setbacks, to appreciate learning in failure, and to anticipate the good that God will bring out of every situation. It's understanding that our thoughts shape our actions, and our actions, in turn, shape our reality.

For the faith-driven entrepreneur, a positive mindset rooted in Christ's promises is not just a personal benefit; it's a testimony of trust in God's sovereignty and goodness.

Action Steps:
1. Mindful Reflection: Begin your day by meditating on Philippians 4:8. Let these virtues guide your thoughts and actions.

2. Gratitude Practice: End your day by listing three positive things that happened, no matter how small, and give thanks for them.

3. Affirmation of Faith: Regularly affirm your trust in God's plan. Speak life into your circumstances, choosing faith-filled optimism over doubt.

Prayer:
Heavenly Father, empower me to choose a positive mindset each day. Help me to fix my thoughts on what is true, noble, and praiseworthy. Let my outlook be shaped by Your promises, and may this perspective influence every aspect of my life and work. Teach me to see my circumstances through the lens of Your goodness and grace. I pray this in Jesus' name, Amen.

Legacy Living: Seeking Generational Impact

"A good person leaves an
inheritance for their
children's children,
but a sinner's wealth is
stored up for the
righteous."

Proverbs 13:22

Day 21

Legacy Living: Seeking Generational Impact

Proverbs 13:22

"A good person leaves an inheritance for their children's children,
but a sinner's wealth is stored up for the righteous."

Reflection:
Legacy isn't about fame, nor is it about achieving short-lived success. True legacy is about planting seeds today that will bear fruit for generations to come. It's about making choices and sacrifices in our present, so our future generations reap the blessings.

The wisdom of Proverbs teaches us that a righteous individual thinks beyond their own lifespan. As faith-driven entrepreneurs, this perspective changes everything. Business decisions are not just about immediate returns; they're about long-term impact. They're about establishing something that endures, that stands the test of time, and that brings honor to God's name.

Legacy living is a powerful reminder to prioritize purpose over profit, eternal significance over ephemeral success. It invites us to consider: What mark are we leaving on the world? How will our efforts today shape the narrative of tomorrow?

Action Steps:
1.Visionary Thinking: Set aside time to envision the long-term impact of your business. How do you want it to be remembered decades or even centuries from now?

2.Intentional Investments: Evaluate where you're investing your resources (time, money, energy). Are these investments aligned with the legacy you want to leave?

3.Mentor and Multiply: Consider how you can mentor the next generation of leaders, imparting to them the wisdom and values that will ensure a lasting legacy.

Prayer:
Lord, help me to see beyond the immediate and into the eternal. Instill in me a heart for legacy, a desire to sow seeds that will bear fruit long after I'm gone. Fruit I may never see. Guide my decisions in light of eternity and let my actions today be a blessing for generations to come. In Jesus' name, Amen.

Schedule a free strategy call with Francine at:
www.consumedcoaching.com

Made in the USA
Columbia, SC
28 March 2025